The Earth is a planet in space. It is a sphere.

D1549330

If you look at the Earth from space you can see land, sea and clouds. You cannot see countries. To see countries you need a map.

0° Equator   0°

Imagine there is a line that goes right round the middle of the Earth. This imaginary line is called the Equator.

Key

Colours show countries.

Transverse Mercator Projection
© Oxford University Press

4 The British Isles

Great Britain and Ireland are islands. They are land with sea all around. These two large islands, together with many smaller ones, make up the British Isles.

This is a picture of the British Isles from space.

This is a map of the British Isles.

Ireland

Isle of Man

Great Britain

Channel Islands

There are two countries in the British Isles. The key shows what the colours and symbols on the map stand for.

Key

United Kingdom

Republic of Ireland

■ capital city

Dublin ■
Republic of Ireland

United Kingdom

London ■

The British Isles are small compared to many places in the world. Can you find the British Isles on a globe?

England, Scotland and Wales together with Northern Ireland make the **United Kingdom**.

Key

England

Scotland

Wales

Northern Ireland

■ capital city

Flags

England

Scotland

Wales

Northern Ireland

Scotland

Edinburgh ■

Northern Ireland
Belfast ■

REPUBLIC OF IRELAND

UNITED KINGDOM

England

Wales

Cardiff ■

London ■

FRANCE

A capital city is the most important city in a country. It is where the government meets. The capital city of the United Kingdom is London.

6 Countries of the world

A country is a land with its own people and its own laws.

Key

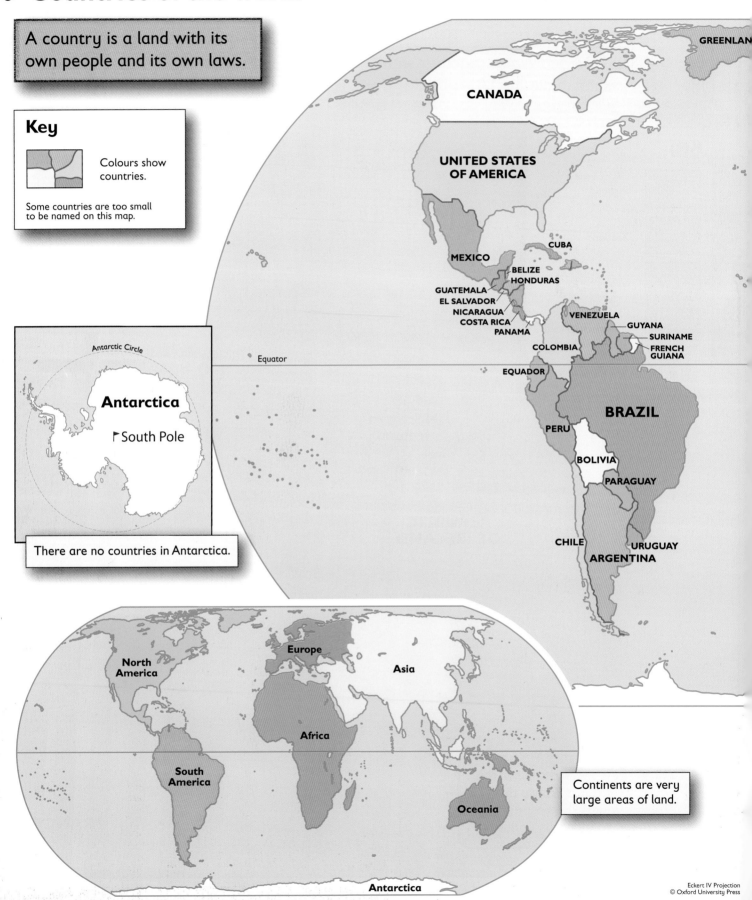

Colours show countries.

Some countries are too small to be named on this map.

Antarctic Circle

Antarctica

᠊South Pole

There are no countries in Antarctica.

Equator

GREENLAND

CANADA

UNITED STATES OF AMERICA

CUBA

MEXICO

BELIZE
HONDURAS

GUATEMALA
EL SALVADOR
NICARAGUA
COSTA RICA
PANAMA

VENEZUELA

GUYANA

SURINAME
FRENCH GUIANA

COLOMBIA

EQUADOR

BRAZIL

PERU

BOLIVIA

PARAGUAY

CHILE

URUGUAY

ARGENTINA

North America

Europe

Asia

Africa

South America

Oceania

Continents are very large areas of land.

Antarctica

Eckert IV Projection
© Oxford University Press

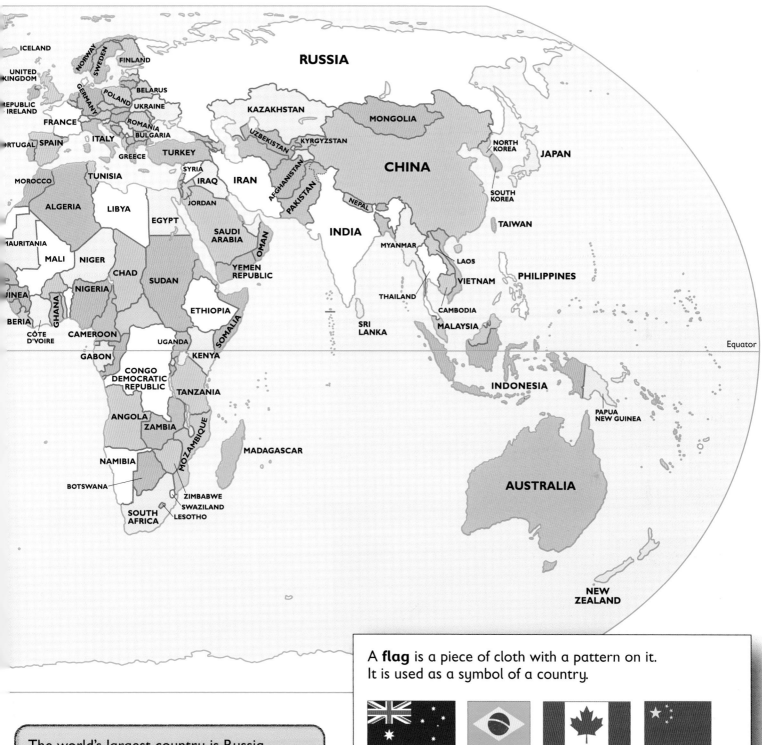

ICELAND
NORWAY
SWEDEN
FINLAND
UNITED KINGDOM
REPUBLIC IRELAND
GERMANY
POLAND
BELARUS
UKRAINE
FRANCE
ROMANIA
BULGARIA
PORTUGAL
SPAIN
ITALY
GREECE
TURKEY
MOROCCO
TUNISIA
SYRIA
IRAQ
IRAN
AFGHANISTAN
PAKISTAN
ALGERIA
LIBYA
JORDAN
EGYPT
MAURITANIA
MALI
NIGER
CHAD
SUDAN
SAUDI ARABIA
OMAN
YEMEN REPUBLIC
GUINEA
NIGERIA
GHANA
LIBERIA
CÔTE D'IVOIRE
CAMEROON
UGANDA
ETHIOPIA
SOMALIA
GABON
KENYA
CONGO DEMOCRATIC REPUBLIC
TANZANIA
ANGOLA
ZAMBIA
MOZAMBIQUE
MADAGASCAR
NAMIBIA
BOTSWANA
ZIMBABWE
SWAZILAND
SOUTH AFRICA
LESOTHO

RUSSIA
KAZAKHSTAN
MONGOLIA
UZBEKISTAN
KYRGYZSTAN
NORTH KOREA
JAPAN
CHINA
SOUTH KOREA
NEPAL
INDIA
TAIWAN
MYANMAR
LAOS
PHILIPPINES
THAILAND
VIETNAM
SRI LANKA
CAMBODIA
MALAYSIA
INDONESIA
PAPUA NEW GUINEA
AUSTRALIA
NEW ZEALAND

Equator

The world's largest country is Russia.
The country with the most people is China.
Can you find Russia and China on the map?

A **flag** is a piece of cloth with a pattern on it.
It is used as a symbol of a country.

Australia

Brazil

Canada

China

India

Russia

United Kingdom

United States of America

Can you find these countries on the map?

8 Mountains, hills and rivers

When you go uphill, the land gets higher. When you go downhill, the land gets lower.

mountains

A mountain is very high land with steep, rocky slopes. Mountains are bigger than hills.

hills

A hill is land that is higher than the land around it. Hills are smaller than mountains.

low land

Land near the sea is low.

rivers

A river is a lot of water that flows down to the sea.

Key

Colours show how high the land is

▲ the highest peaks

mountains

hills

low land

~~~ rivers

ATLANTIC OCEAN

NORTHWEST HIGHLANDS

Great Glen

River Spey

River Dee

GRAMPIAN MOUNTAINS

Ben Nevis ▲

River Clyde

North Sea

River Tweed

SOUTHERN UPLANDS

River Tyne

Lake District

▲ Scafell Pike

PENNINES

North York Moors

River Aire

Antrim Mountains

River Bann

Loch Neagh

Slieve Donard ▲

River Erne

Irish Sea

Loch Corrib

River Shannon

River Liffey

Wicklow Mountains

River Barrow

River Blackwater

▲ Carrantuohill

Snowdon ▲

River Severn

River Trent

CAMBRIAN MOUNTAINS

River Wye

River Avon

River Great Ouse

Brecon Beacons

Cotswold Hills

Chiltern Hills

River Thames

North Downs

South Downs

Exmoor

Dartmoor

English Channel

The highest mountain in the British Isles is Ben Nevis.
Can you find it on the map?

The longest river in the British Isles is the River Shannon.
Can you find it on the map?

Transverse Mercator Projection
© Oxford University Press

10 Mountains and rivers around the world

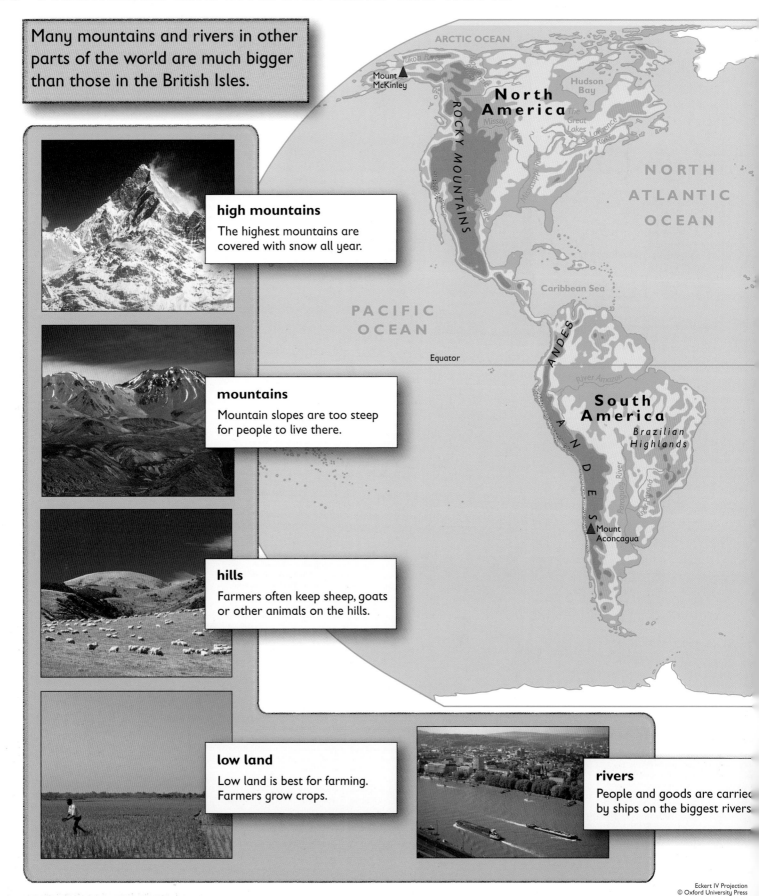

Many mountains and rivers in other parts of the world are much bigger than those in the British Isles.

high mountains
The highest mountains are covered with snow all year.

mountains
Mountain slopes are too steep for people to live there.

hills
Farmers often keep sheep, goats or other animals on the hills.

low land
Low land is best for farming. Farmers grow crops.

rivers
People and goods are carried by ships on the biggest rivers

ARCTIC OCEAN

Yukon River

Mount McKinley

North America

ROCKY MOUNTAINS

Hudson Bay

The Great Lakes

St Lawrence River

Missouri R.

Rio Grande

Mississippi R.

NORTH ATLANTIC OCEAN

Caribbean Sea

PACIFIC OCEAN

Equator

ANDES

River Amazon

South America

Brazilian Highlands

Paraguay River

River Paraná

Mount Aconcagua

Eckert IV Projection
© Oxford University Press

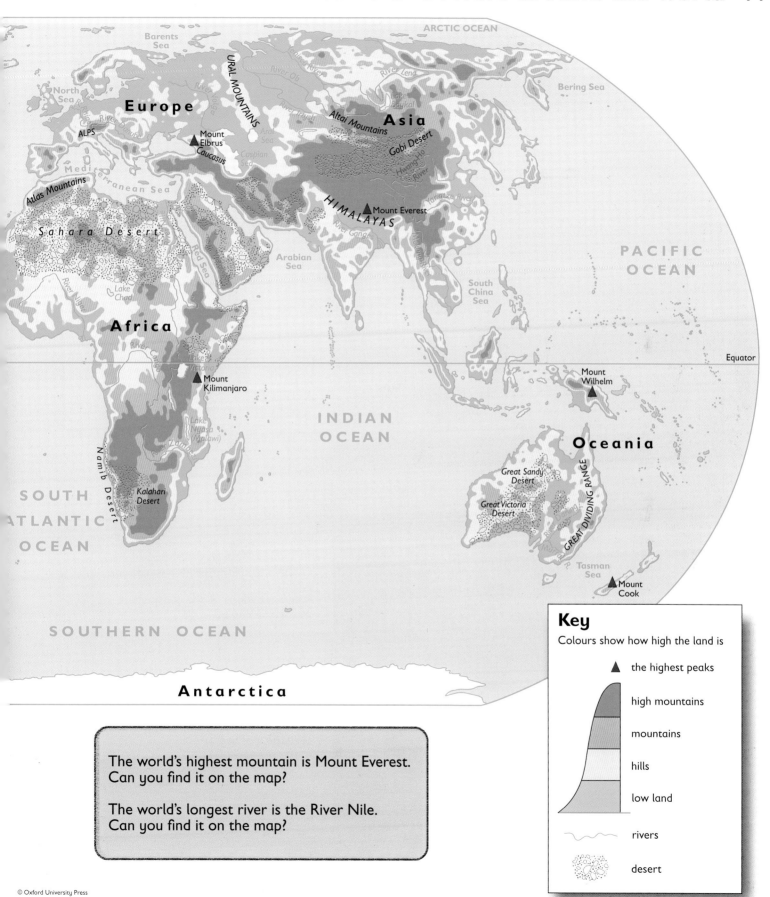

ARCTIC OCEAN

Barents Sea

North Sea

Europe

URAL MOUNTAINS

ALPS

River Volga

Mount Elbrus
Caucasus

River Danube

Mediterranean Sea

Atlas Mountains

Sahara Desert

Red Sea

River Niger

Lake Chad

Africa

River Congo

Lake Victoria

▲ Mount Kilimanjaro

River Zambezi

Lake Ngasa (Malawi)

Namib Desert

Kalahari Desert

SOUTH ATLANTIC OCEAN

River Ob

River Irtysh

Aral Sea

Caspian Sea

Arabian Sea

River Ob

River Yenisey

River Lena

Lake Baykal

Bering Sea

Altai Mountains

Asia

Gobi Desert

Hwang-Ho River

HIMALAYAS

▲ Mount Everest

River Ganges

Yangtze River

South China Sea

PACIFIC OCEAN

Equator

Mount Wilhelm ▲

INDIAN OCEAN

Oceania

Great Sandy Desert

Great Victoria Desert

GREAT DIVIDING RANGE

Tasman Sea

▲ Mount Cook

SOUTHERN OCEAN

Antarctica

The world's highest mountain is Mount Everest.
Can you find it on the map?

The world's longest river is the River Nile.
Can you find it on the map?

Key

Colours show how high the land is

▲ the highest peaks

high mountains

mountains

hills

low land

~~~ rivers

∴∴∴ desert

12 By the sea

Where the land meets the sea is called the **coast**.

beach

A beach is land by the edge of the sea that is covered with sand or small stones.

cliff

A cliff is a hill with one side that goes straight down to the sea.

port

A port is a place on the coast where ships come and go.

seaside resort

A seaside resort is a place where you go for a seaside holiday.

By the sea in the United Kingdom

Key

	sandy beaches
	cliffs
⚓	port
⛱	seaside resort
	river

Scotland

Forth

River Spey

River Dee

River Clyde

River Tweed

North Sea

Stranraer

River Tyne — Tyne

Tees and Hartlepool

Whitby

Scarborough

Northern Ireland

Belfast

Heysham

Bridlington

Blackpool

River Aire

Hull

ATLANTIC OCEAN

Irish Sea

Llandudno

Liverpool

England

Grimsby and Illingham

Holyhead

Skegness

River Trent

River Severn

Great Yarmouth

Wales

River Wye

River Avon

River Great Ouse

Felixstowe

Milford Haven

River Thames

Southend-on-Sea

Ilfracombe

London

Dover

Southampton Portsmouth

Brighton

Weymouth

Eastbourne

St. Ives

Torquay

Newhaven

Plymouth

English Channel

What was the seaside like in the past?
How does the seaside look
different today?

14 Our weather

The weather is how it is outside, for example, whether it is hot or cold, sunny or raining.

spring			summer			autumn			winter		
March	April	May	June	July	August	September	October	November	December	January	February

The year has twelve months and four seasons.

Our summers are usually warm or hot.
Our winters are usually cool or cold.

The weather is slightly different from place to place in the British Isles.

The **north** has more cold days.

The **west** has more rainy days.

north

west

east

south

The **east** has more dry, sunny days.

The **south** has more warm days.

The weather in the British Isles

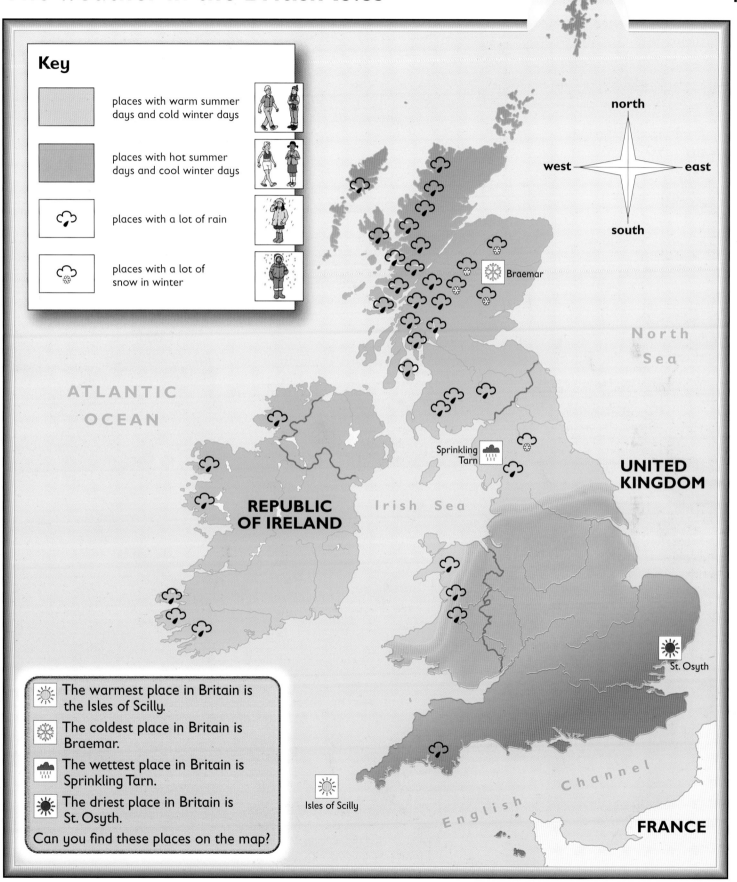

Key

- places with warm summer days and cold winter days
- places with hot summer days and cool winter days
- places with a lot of rain
- places with a lot of snow in winter

north
west — east
south

ATLANTIC OCEAN

North Sea

Braemar

Sprinkling Tarn

REPUBLIC OF IRELAND

Irish Sea

UNITED KINGDOM

St. Osyth

English Channel

Isles of Scilly

FRANCE

- The warmest place in Britain is the Isles of Scilly.
- The coldest place in Britain is Braemar.
- The wettest place in Britain is Sprinkling Tarn.
- The driest place in Britain is St. Osyth.

Can you find these places on the map?

16 Weather around the world

Homes and clothes around the world are designed according to what the weather is usually like.

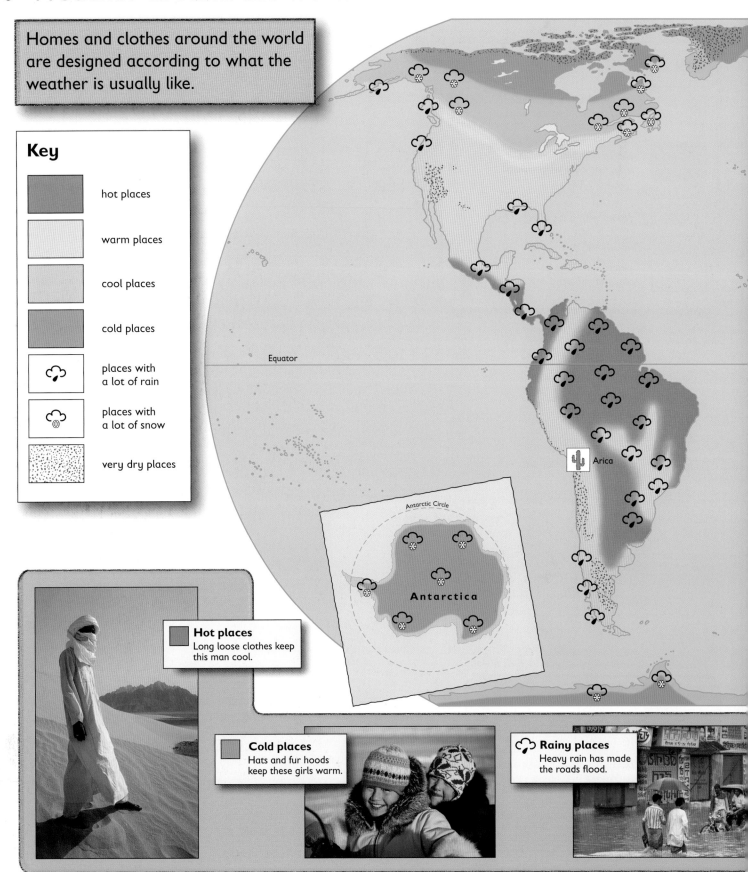

Key

■	hot places
▢	warm places
▢	cool places
▢	cold places
☁	places with a lot of rain
☁	places with a lot of snow
⬚	very dry places

Equator

Arica

Antarctic Circle

Antarctica

Hot places
Long loose clothes keep this man cool.

Cold places
Hats and fur hoods keep these girls warm.

Rainy places
Heavy rain has made the roads flood.

Eckert IV Projection
© Oxford University Press

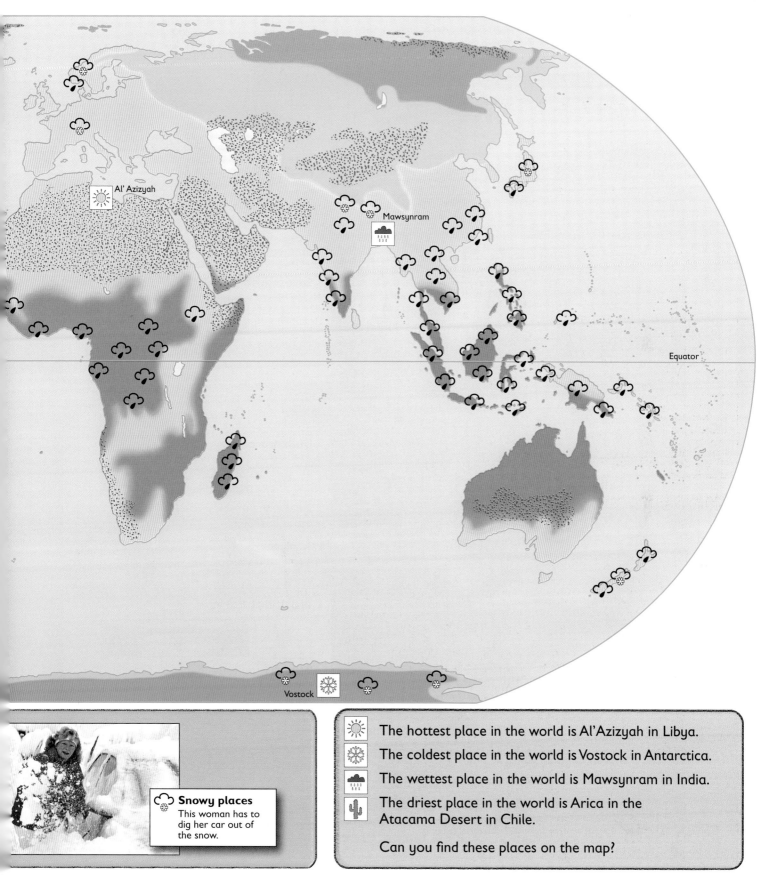

Al' Azizyah

Mawsynram

Equator

Vostock

Snowy places
This woman has to dig her car out of the snow.

The hottest place in the world is Al'Azizyah in Libya.

The coldest place in the world is Vostock in Antarctica.

The wettest place in the world is Mawsynram in India.

The driest place in the world is Arica in the Atacama Desert in Chile.

Can you find these places on the map?

18 Our environment

The environment is the air, land and water that surrounds us. We need to protect the environment.

farmland

Farmers use the land to produce food by growing crops and keeping animals.

forest and woodland

Land used to grow trees for wood.

built-up areas

Land with houses, shops, factories and other buildings.

National Parks

Beautiful countryside that is specially protected.

Heritage Coast

Beautiful coastal scenery that is specially protected.

Environments in the United Kingdom

Key

- farmland
- forest and woodland
- built-up areas
- National Parks
- Heritage Coast

ATLANTIC OCEAN

North Sea

Scotland
- Cairngorms
- Aberdeen
- Dundee
- The Trossachs
- Loch Lomond
- Edinburgh
- Glasgow

Northern Ireland
- Belfast

Irish Sea

- Northumberland
- Newcastle upon Tyne
- Middlesbrough
- Lake District
- North York Moors
- Yorkshire Dales
- Leeds
- Kingston upon Hull
- Liverpool
- Manchester
- Sheffield
- Peak District

England

Wales
- Snowdonia
- Pembrokeshire Coast
- Brecon Beacons
- Cardiff
- Bristol
- Birmingham
- Leicester
- Norwich
- The Broads
- London
- Exmoor
- Southampton
- New Forest
- South Downs
- Dartmoor

English Channel

Most National Parks have hills or mountains.

Which is the nearest National Park to where you live?

Transverse Mercator Projection
© Oxford University Press

There are different environments around the world. In some places there are very many plants, in others very few.

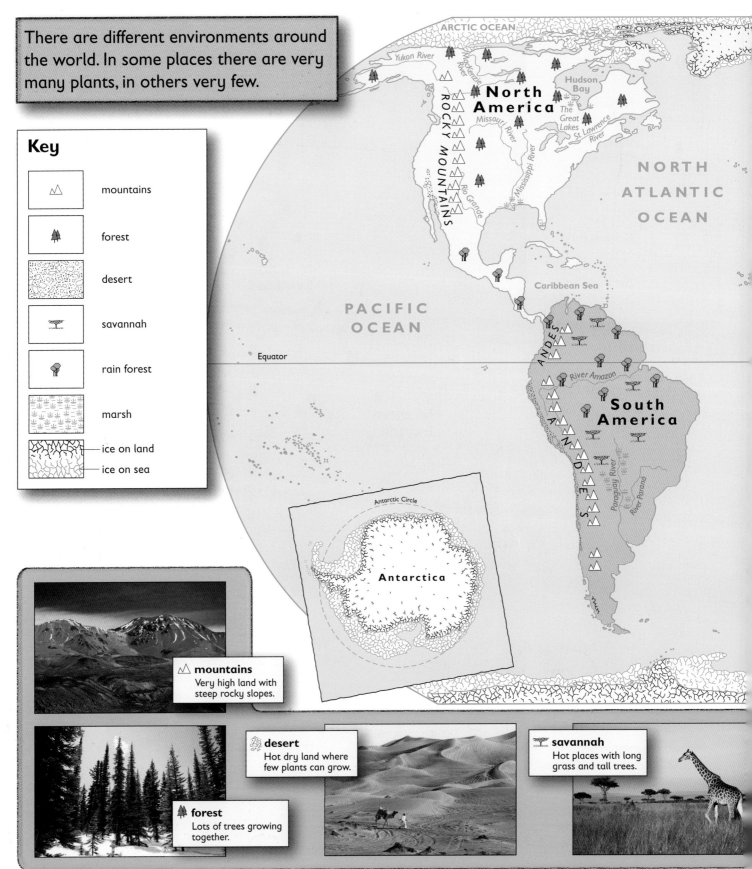

Key

△△	mountains
🌲	forest
(dotted)	desert
🌴	savannah
🌳	rain forest
(marsh symbol)	marsh
(ice symbol)	ice on land — ice on sea

ARCTIC OCEAN

Yukon River
Mackenzie River

North America

Hudson Bay

ROCKY MOUNTAINS

Missouri River

The Great Lakes

St Lawrence River

Rio Grande

Mississippi River

NORTH ATLANTIC OCEAN

PACIFIC OCEAN

Caribbean Sea

Equator

ANDES

River Amazon

South America

Paraguay River

River Paraná

Antarctic Circle

Antarctica

△△ **mountains**
Very high land with steep rocky slopes.

🌲 **forest**
Lots of trees growing together.

desert
Hot dry land where few plants can grow.

🌴 **savannah**
Hot places with long grass and tall trees.

Eckert IV Projection
© Oxford University Press

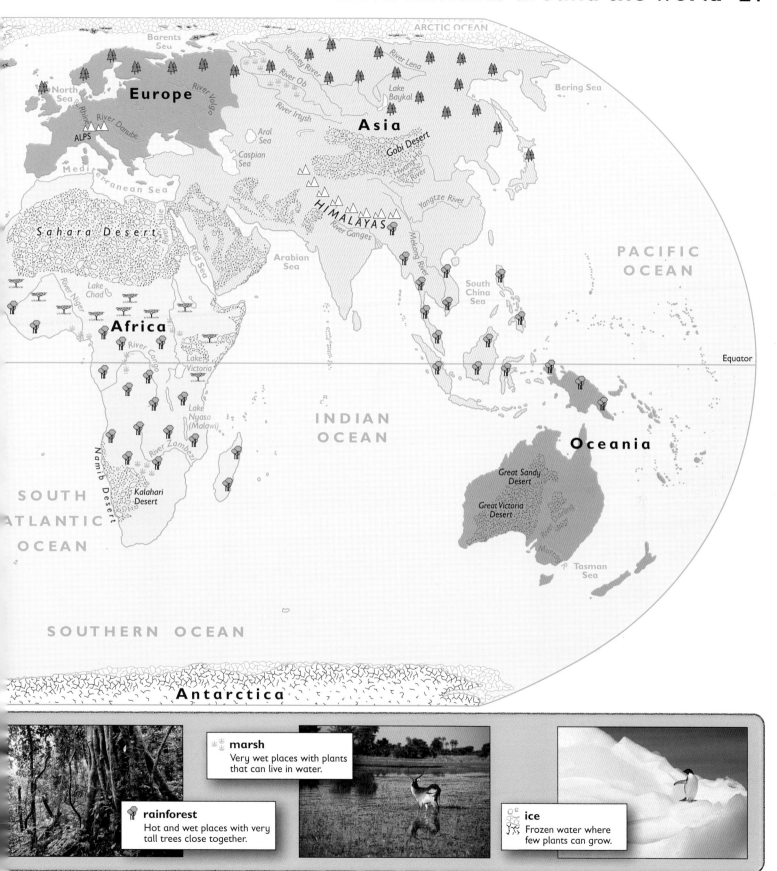

ARCTIC OCEAN

Barents Sea

Europe

North Sea

River Rhine
River Danube
ALPS

River Volga

Yenisey River
River Ob

River Lena

River Irtysh

Bering Sea

Asia

Aral Sea

Caspian Sea

Lake Baykal

Gobi Desert

Hwang-Ho River

HIMALAYAS

Yangtze River

River Nile

Red Sea

River Ganges

Mekong River

Sahara Desert

Arabian Sea

River Niger

Lake Chad

Africa

River Congo

Lake Victoria

Lake Nyasa (Malawi)

River Zambezi

Namib Desert

Kalahari Desert

PACIFIC OCEAN

South China Sea

Equator

Oceania

INDIAN OCEAN

Great Sandy Desert

Great Victoria Desert

River Darling

River Murray

Tasman Sea

SOUTH ATLANTIC OCEAN

SOUTHERN OCEAN

Antarctica

marsh
Very wet places with plants that can live in water.

rainforest
Hot and wet places with very tall trees close together.

ice
Frozen water where few plants can grow.

© Oxford University Press

22 Animals around the world

Each of these animals is suited to the environment in which it lives. If the environment changes, animals may die.

Key

	fox
	squirrel
	camel
	panda
	tiger
	giraffe
	howler monkey
	Andean condor
	polar bear
	kangaroo
	crocodile
	penguin
	whale
	bobcat
	grey wolf

ARCTIC OCEAN

Yukon River
Mackenzie River

North America

Hudson Bay

ROCKY MOUNTAINS

The Great Lakes
St Lawrence River

Missouri River
Mississippi River
Rio Grande

NORTH ATLANTIC OCEAN

PACIFIC OCEAN

Caribbean Sea

Equator

ANDES

River Amazon

South America

Paraguay River
Paraná

A N D E S

Antarctic Circle

Antarctica

Grey wolf

Kangaroo

Eckert IV Projection
© Oxford University Press

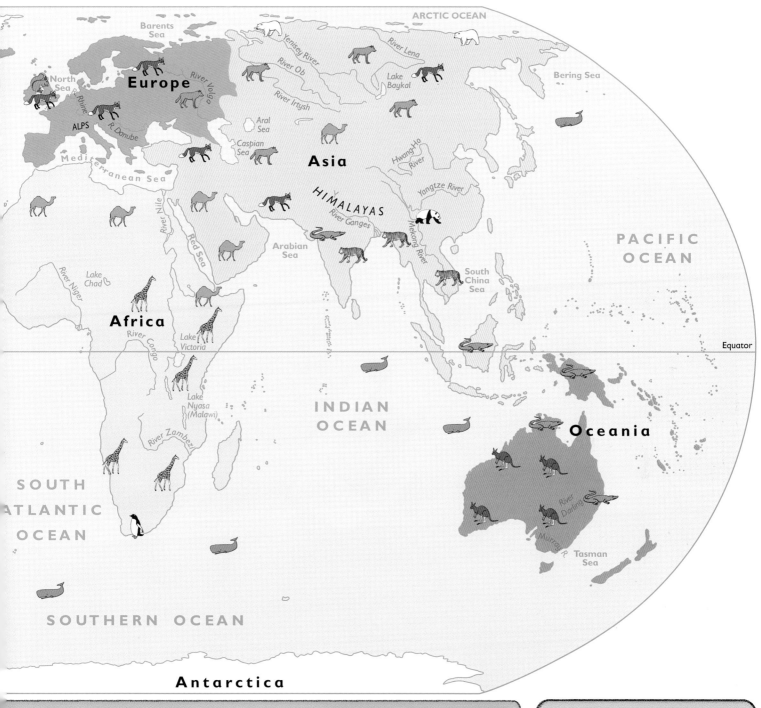

Tiger

Panda

Choose an animal from each continent.

Can you say why it is especially suited to its environment?

24 Towns and cities

A town is a place with a lot of houses, shops, factories, offices and other buildings. A city is a very large town. Towns and cities are built-up areas.

built-up area

This photograph shows part of Birmingham seen from the air. Can you find:

• A street with houses
• A football stadium
• A main road
• A park
• A carpark
• A railway line

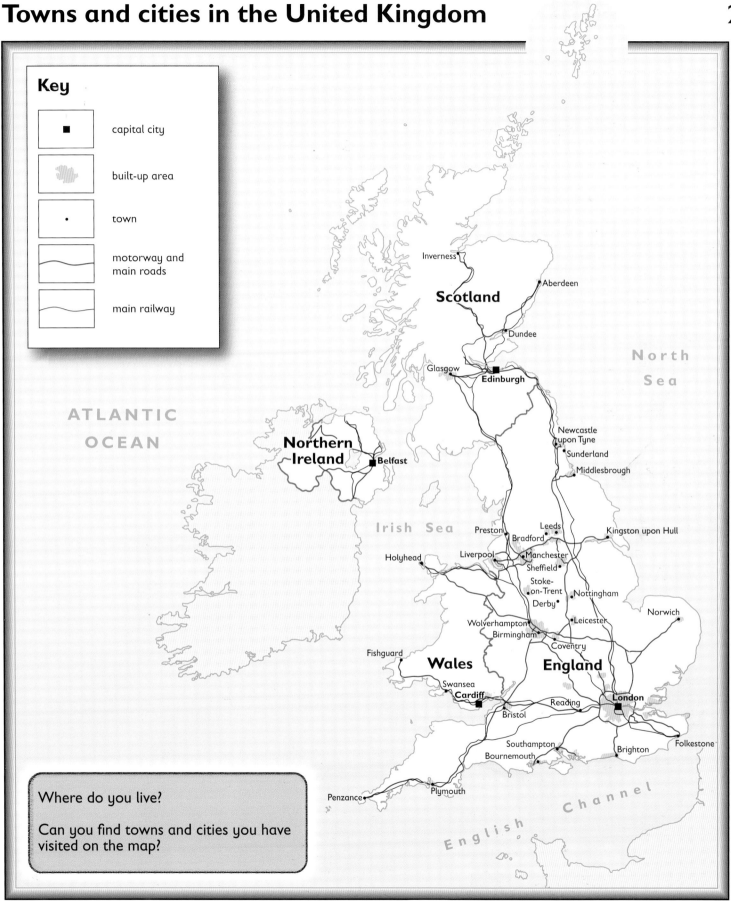

Key

■ capital city

built-up area

• town

motorway and main roads

main railway

ATLANTIC OCEAN

Inverness

Scotland

Aberdeen

Dundee

Glasgow

Edinburgh

North Sea

Northern Ireland

Belfast

Newcastle upon Tyne

Sunderland

Middlesbrough

Irish Sea

Preston

Leeds

Bradford

Kingston upon Hull

Holyhead

Liverpool

Manchester

Sheffield

Stoke-on-Trent

Nottingham

Derby

Norwich

Wolverhampton

Leicester

Birmingham

Coventry

Fishguard

Wales

England

Swansea

Cardiff

Reading

London

Bristol

Southampton

Brighton

Folkestone

Bournemouth

Penzance

Plymouth

English Channel

Where do you live?

Can you find towns and cities you have visited on the map?

Some places in the world are very crowded. Other places have very few people.

Key

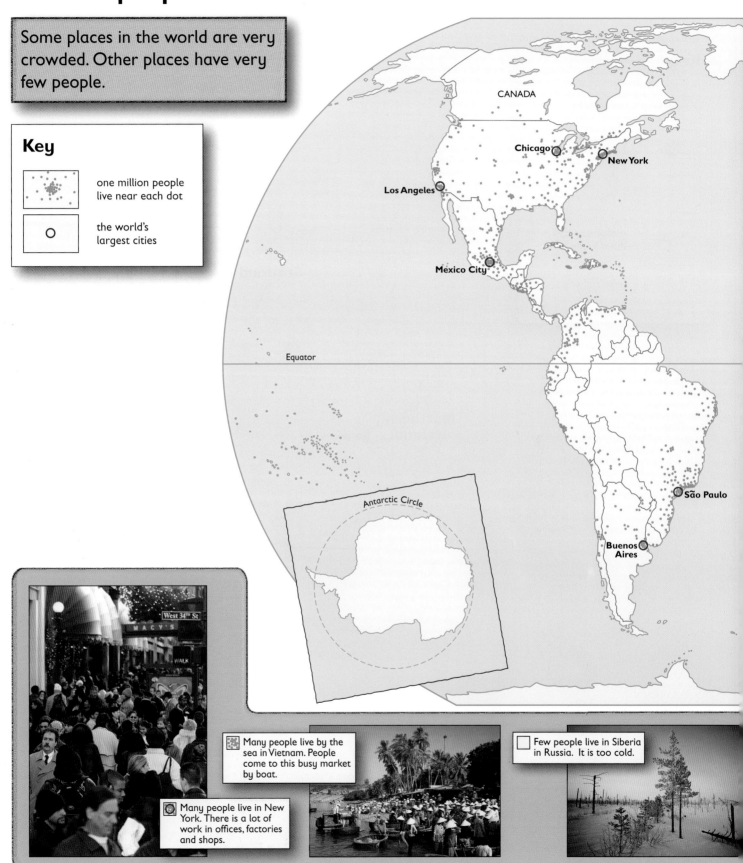

one million people live near each dot

the world's largest cities

CANADA

Chicago
New York
Los Angeles
Mexico City
São Paulo
Buenos Aires

Equator

Antarctic Circle

Many people live by the sea in Vietnam. People come to this busy market by boat.

Many people live in New York. There is a lot of work in offices, factories and shops.

Few people live in Siberia in Russia. It is too cold.

Eckert IV Projection
© Oxford University Press

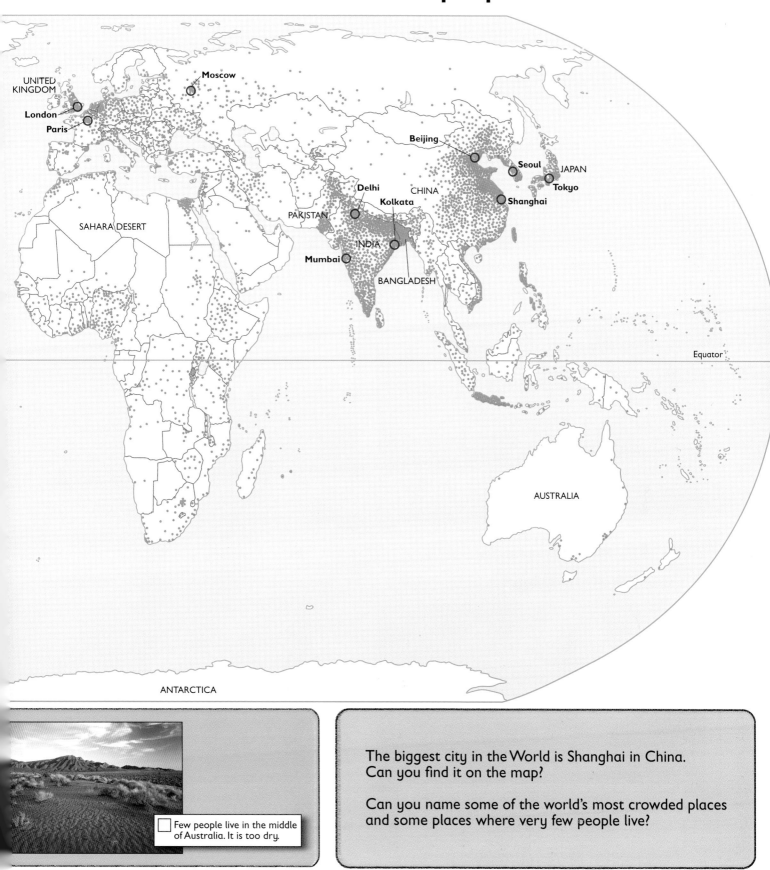

UNITED KINGDOM

Moscow

London

Paris

SAHARA DESERT

Beijing

CHINA

Seoul

JAPAN

Tokyo

Delhi

Shanghai

Kolkata

PAKISTAN

INDIA

Mumbai

BANGLADESH

Equator

AUSTRALIA

ANTARCTICA

Few people live in the middle of Australia. It is too dry.

The biggest city in the World is Shanghai in China. Can you find it on the map?

Can you name some of the world's most crowded places and some places where very few people live?

Holidays are time off from school or work. What is there to see and do near where you live?

Castles are large strong buildings with thick stone walls and tall towers. They were built long ago to keep people safe from their enemies.

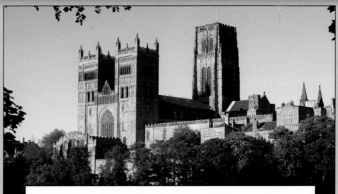

Cathedrals are big churches that were built by Christians to worship God.

Museums are places where interesting things are kept for people to go and see.

Theme parks are very large outdoor play areas with exciting rides.

Zoos are places where wild animals are kept so that people can go and see them up close.

Some parts of the **countryside and coast** are especially beautiful and many people go on holiday to enjoy the views.

Holidays in the United Kingdom

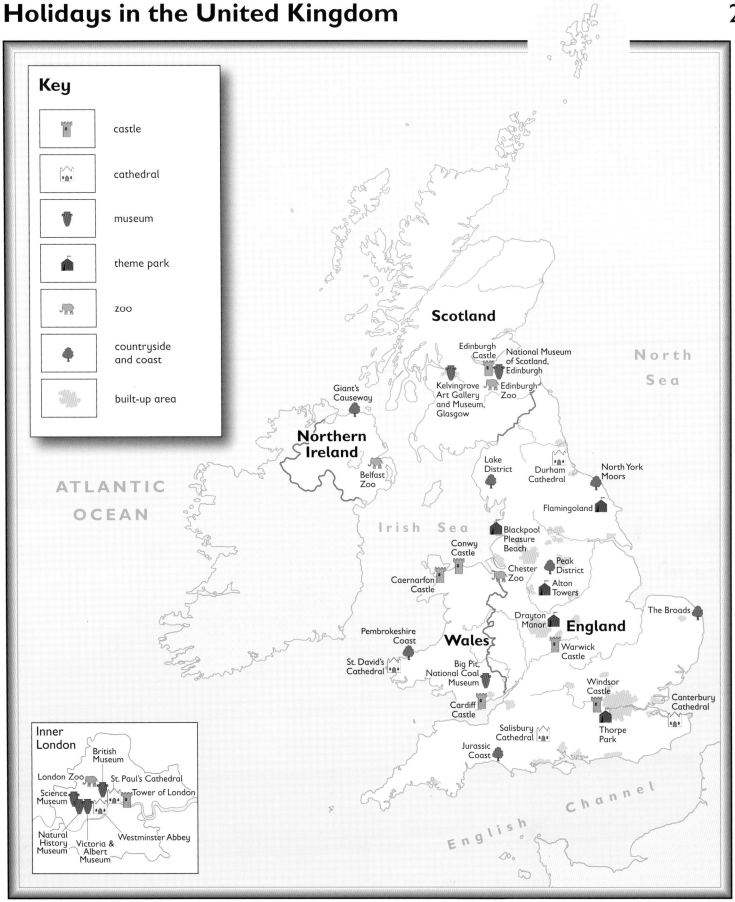

Key

castle	
cathedral	
museum	
theme park	
zoo	
countryside and coast	
built-up area	

Scotland

Edinburgh Castle
National Museum of Scotland, Edinburgh
Kelvingrove Art Gallery and Museum, Glasgow
Edinburgh Zoo

Northern Ireland

Giant's Causeway
Belfast Zoo

ATLANTIC OCEAN

Irish Sea

North Sea

Lake District
Durham Cathedral
North York Moors
Flamingoland
Blackpool Pleasure Beach
Peak District
Conwy Castle
Chester Zoo
Alton Towers
Caernarfon Castle

Wales

England

Pembrokeshire Coast
Drayton Manor
The Broads
Warwick Castle
St. David's Cathedral
Big Pit, National Coal Museum
Windsor Castle
Canterbury Cathedral
Cardiff Castle
Thorpe Park
Salisbury Cathedral
Jurassic Coast

English Channel

Inner London

British Museum
London Zoo
St. Paul's Cathedral
Science Museum
Tower of London
Natural History Museum
Victoria & Albert Museum
Westminster Abbey

A passport is a booklet that shows who you are and what country you come from. You need a passport to travel to other countries. Here are some places in the world you might like to visit.

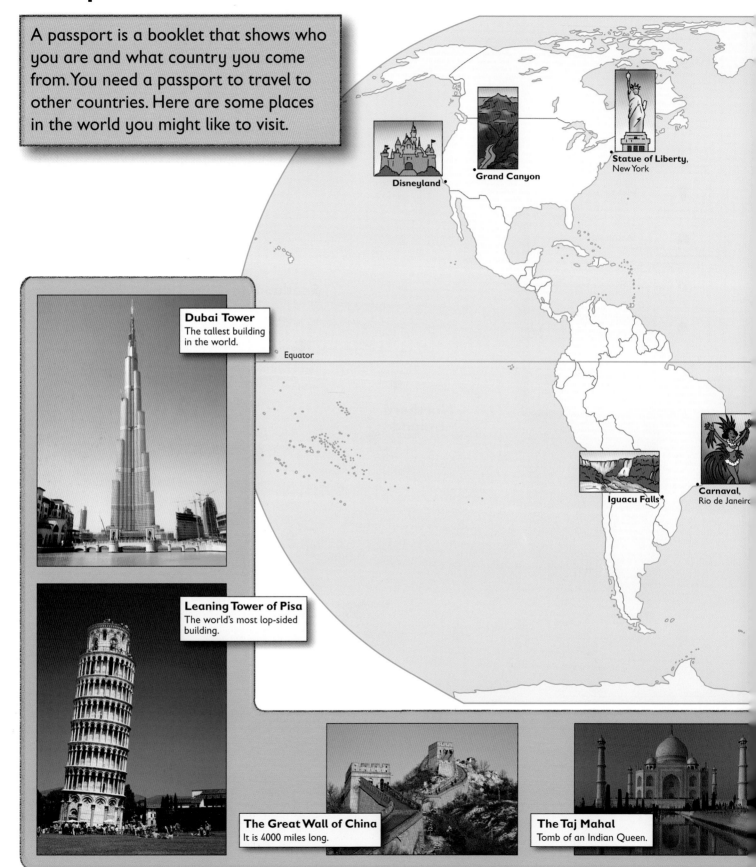

Disneyland

Grand Canyon

Statue of Liberty, New York

Equator

Iguacu Falls

Carnaval, Rio de Janeiro

Dubai Tower
The tallest building in the world.

Leaning Tower of Pisa
The world's most lop-sided building.

The Great Wall of China
It is 4000 miles long.

The Taj Mahal
Tomb of an Indian Queen.

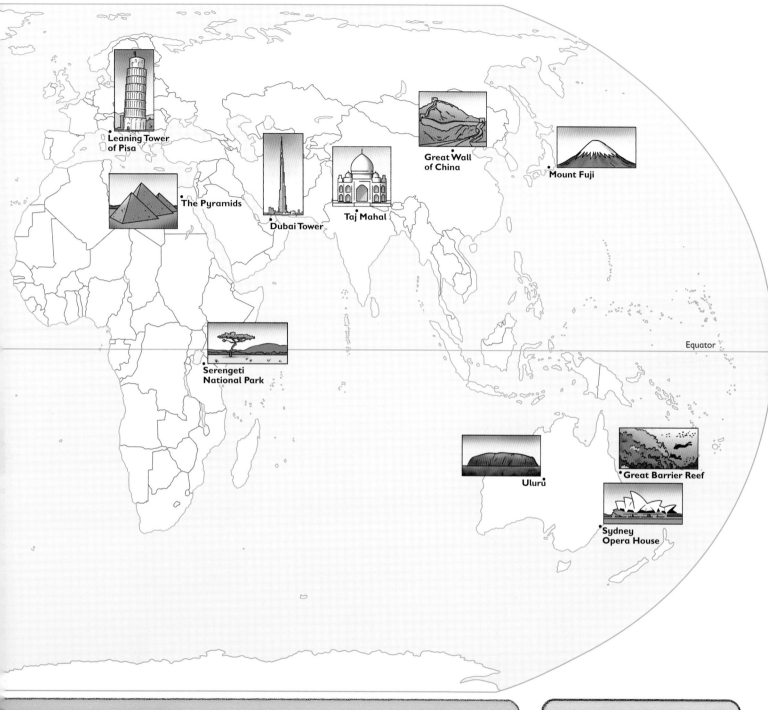

Leaning Tower of Pisa

The Pyramids

Dubai Tower

Taj Mahal

Great Wall of China

Mount Fuji

Serengeti National Park

Equator

Uluru

Great Barrier Reef

Sydney Opera House

Mount Fuji
A volcano covered in snow.

The Grand Canyon
It is more than a mile deep.

Where in the world would you like to go?

How will you get there?

What will it be like when you are there?

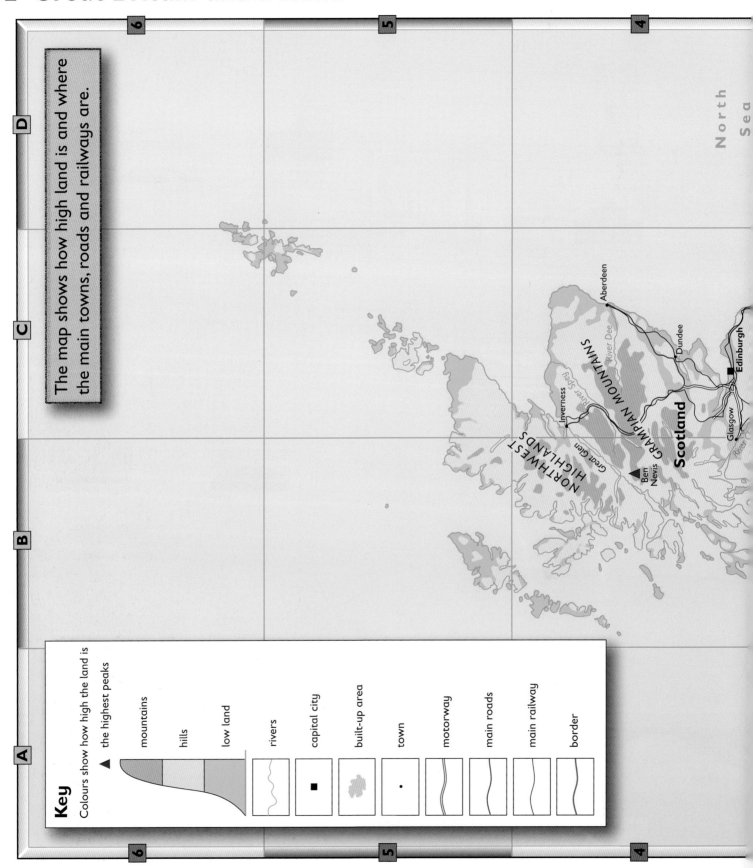

The map shows how high land is and where the main towns, roads and railways are.

Key

Colours show how high the land is

▲ the highest peaks

- mountains
- hills
- low land

- rivers
- capital city ■
- built-up area
- town ·
- motorway
- main roads
- main railway
- border

North Sea

Aberdeen

River Dee

Dundee

River Spey

GRAMPIAN MOUNTAINS

Inverness

Edinburgh ■

Great Glen

NORTHWEST HIGHLANDS

Ben Nevis ▲

Scotland

Glasgow

River

Transverse Mercator Projection
© Oxford University Press

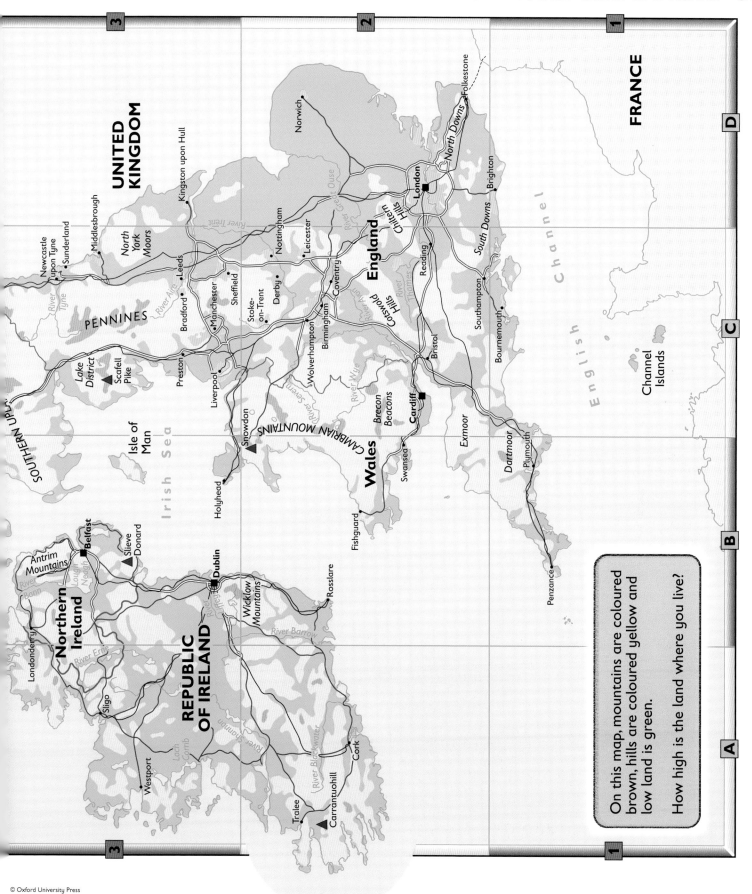

FRANCE

UNITED KINGDOM

England

Wales

Northern Ireland

REPUBLIC OF IRELAND

PENNINES

SOUTHERN UPLANDS

CAMBRIAN MOUNTAINS

Folkestone
Norwich
London
Brighton
Kingston upon Hull
Middlesbrough
North York Moors
Sunderland
Newcastle upon Tyne
Leeds
Bradford
Manchester
Sheffield
Nottingham
Leicester
Derby
Stoke-on-Trent
Coventry
Birmingham
Wolverhampton
Preston
Liverpool
Reading
Southampton
Bournemouth
Bristol
Cardiff
Swansea
Exmoor
Dartmoor
Plymouth
Penzance
Fishguard
Holyhead
Snowdon
Lake District
Scafell Pike
Isle of Man
Chiltern Hills
Cotswold Hills
North Downs
South Downs
Brecon Beacons

River Trent
River Great Ouse
River Thames
River Avon
River Wye
River Severn
River Aire
River Tyne

English Channel

Channel Islands

Irish Sea

Belfast
Slieve Donard
Antrim Mountains
Londonderry
Sligo
Westport
Tralee
Cork
Carrantuohill
Dublin
Rosslare
Wicklow Mountains

Lough Neagh
River Bann
River Erne
River Blackwater
River Shannon
Lough Corrib
River Barrow
River Liffey

On this map, mountains are coloured brown, hills are coloured yellow and low land is green.

How high is the land where you live?

ICELAND
■ Reykjavik

SWEDEN

FINLAND

NORWAY
■ Oslo

Stockholm

Helsinki
■
St. Petersbu
Tallinn
ESTONIA

North
Sea

DENMARK

Riga
■ LATVIA

LITHUANIA

Copenhagen
Vilnius
■

UNITED
KINGDOM

Minsk
■

REPUBLIC
OF IRELAND

Dublin ■

NETHERLANDS

Berlin
■

POLAND

BELARU

Amsterdam

GERMANY

Warsaw
■

London ■

Brussels
BELGIUM

River Rhine

LUXEMBOURG

ATLANTIC

Prague
■ CZECH
REPUBLIC

SLOVAKIA

UKRAINE

OCEAN

Paris
■

River Seine

Vienna
■

Bratislava

River Danube

FRANCE

Bern ■
SWITZERLAND

AUSTRIA

Budapest
■

HUNGARY

MOLDO
Chişinău
■

Mont
Blanc

Ljubljana
■ SLOVENIA

Zagreb
■ CROATIA

ROMANIA

Alps

BOSNIA-
HERZEGOVINA

Belgrade
■

Bucharest
■

Pyrenées

Corsica

Sarajevo ■

SERBIA

ITALY

MONTENEGRO

BULGARIA

Madrid
■

Podgorica
■

KOSOVO

■ Sofia

MACEDONIA

PORTUGAL

Rome
■

Sardinia

Tiranë ■
ALBANIA

Skopje
■

Istanbu

SPAIN

Majorca

GREECE

Lisbon ■

Mediterranean Sea

Sicily

MALTA

Athens
■

Crete

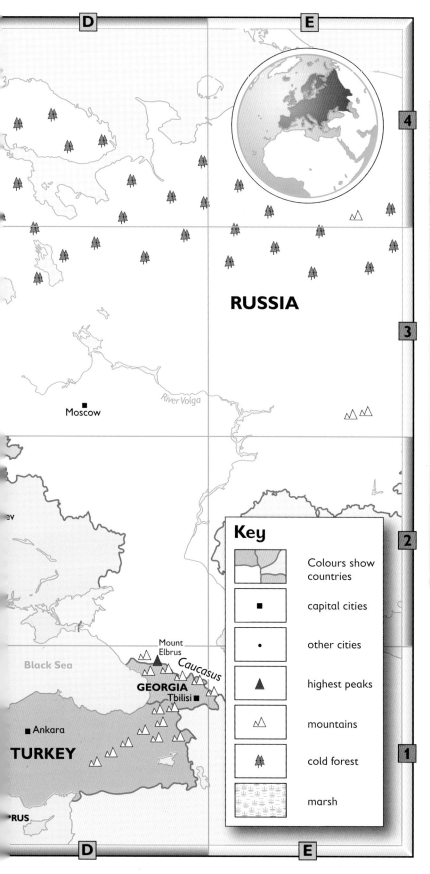

Key

(colours)	Colours show countries
■	capital cities
•	other cities
▲	highest peaks
⌃⌃	mountains
🌲	cold forest
(marsh pattern)	marsh

RUSSIA

Moscow

River Volga

Black Sea

Mount Elbrus

Caucasus

GEORGIA

Tbilisi

Ankara

TURKEY

CYPRUS

D   E

4   3   2   1

There are many European languages.

Many people go on holiday to Spain because the weather in summer is hot and dry.

Painted Easter eggs are popular in many European countries.

Do you know what language people speak in each of these countries?

France
Spain
Greece
Italy
The Netherlands

36 Asia

RUSSIA

River Volga
River Ob
River Irtysh
Yenisey River
River Lena

Moscow

KAZAKHSTAN
Astana

Altai Mountains
Ulan Bator
MONGOLIA

Gobi Desert

ARMENIA
Baku
Yerevan
AZERBAIJAN
Caspian Sea
UZBEKISTAN
Tashkent
Bishkek
KYRGYZSTAN

Beijing

NORTH
KOREA
Pyongyan

TURKMENISTAN
Ashgabat
TAJIKISTAN
Dushanbe
Mount K2

CHINA

SOU
KOR
Seoul

Tehran

AFGHANISTAN
Kabul

Hwang-Ho River

SYRIA
Damascus
Beirut
Baghdad
LEBANON
ISRAEL
IRAQ
Jerusalem
Amman
JORDAN
IRAN
Islamabad

Himalayas

Shanghai

Yangtze River

NEPAL
Mount
Everest
Thimphu
BHUTAN

New
Delhi
River Ganges
Kathmandu

Mekong River

KUWAIT
Kuwait
City
PAKISTAN

QATAR
Riyadh
UNITED
ARAB
EMIRATES
Muscat

BANGLADESH
Dhaka
Kolkata

Taipei

TAIWAN

SAUDI
ARABIA
OMAN

INDIA

MYANMAR
Hanoi
Hong
Kong

Mumbai
Yangon
LAOS
Vientiane

SANA
YEMEN
Sana

THAILAND
Bangkok
CAMBODIA
Phnom
Penh
VIETNAM
Manila
PHILIPPINES

SRI
LANKA
Colombo

MALAYSIA
BRUNEI
Bandar Seri Begawan
Kuala Lumpur

SINGAPORE

INDIAN

OCEAN

Jakarta
INDONESIA
Dili
EAST
TIMOR

How big is Asia?

Compare with the
British Isles.

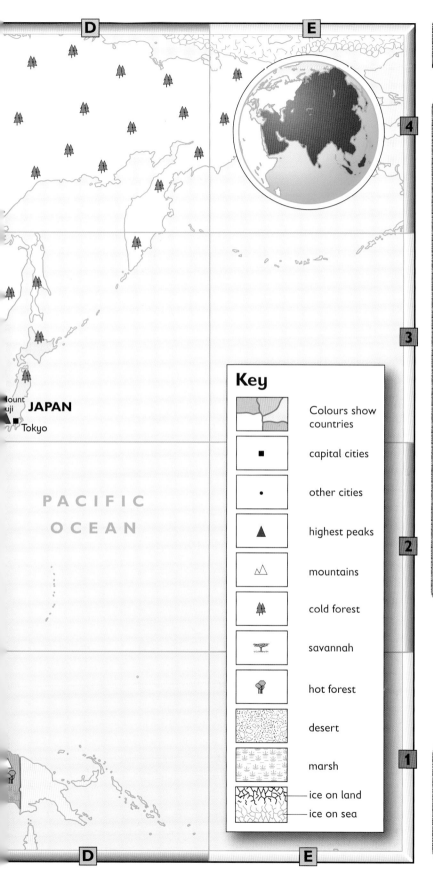

JAPAN

Tokyo

Mount uji

PACIFIC
OCEAN

Key

	Colours show countries
■	capital cities
•	other cities
▲	highest peaks
⌒	mountains
🌲	cold forest
	savannah
🌳	hot forest
	desert
	marsh
	ice on land
	ice on sea

Asia is the largest continent.

It takes a whole week to travel across Russia by train.

In China and Japan people eat with chopsticks.

Russia is the largest country in the world. Can you find Russia on the map?

China has more people than any other country. Can you find China on the map?

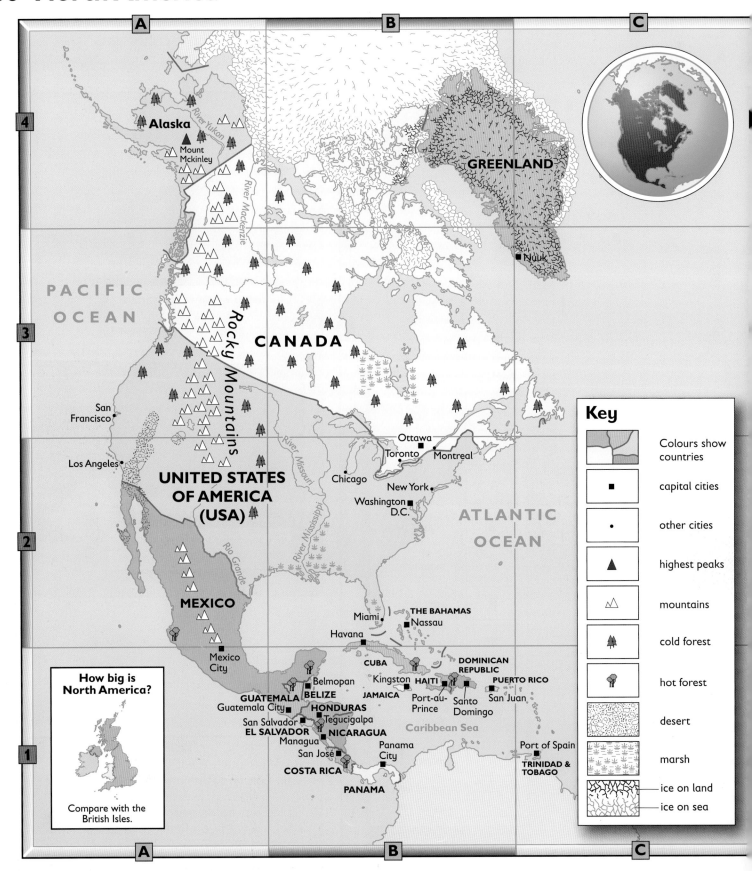

Key

	Colours show countries
	capital cities
	other cities
	highest peaks
	mountains
	cold forest
	hot forest
	desert
	marsh
	ice on land
	ice on sea

How big is North America?

Compare with the British Isles.

PACIFIC OCEAN

Alaska
Mount Mckinley
River Yukon
River Mackenzie
Rocky Mountains
CANADA
GREENLAND
Nuuk

San Francisco
Los Angeles
UNITED STATES OF AMERICA (USA)
River Missouri
River Mississippi
Rio Grande
Chicago
Ottawa
Toronto
Montreal
New York
Washington D.C.
ATLANTIC OCEAN

MEXICO
Mexico City

Miami
THE BAHAMAS
Nassau
Havana
CUBA
Kingston
JAMAICA
HAITI
Port-au-Prince
DOMINICAN REPUBLIC
Santo Domingo
PUERTO RICO
San Juan
Caribbean Sea

Belmopan
BELIZE
GUATEMALA
Guatemala City
HONDURAS
Tegucigalpa
San Salvador
EL SALVADOR
NICARAGUA
Managua
San José
COSTA RICA
Panama City
PANAMA
Port of Spain
TRINIDAD & TOBAGO

The United States of America is the richest country in the world.

Mexico is famous for its spicy food.

The Statue of Liberty stands in New York harbour.

School buses in the United States and Canada are painted yellow.

The president of the United States lives in the White House.

SCHOOL BUS

74

74

The capital of the United States is Washington D.C. Can you find it on the map?

40 South America

Key

(colours)	Colours show countries
■	capital cities
•	other cities
▲	highest peaks
⋀	mountains
🌳	savannah
🌲	hot forest
(dots)	desert
(marks)	marsh

How big is South America?

Compare with the British Isles.

PACIFIC OCEAN

ATLANTIC OCEAN

Caracas

VENEZUELA

Georgetown

Paramaribo
Cayenne

SURINAME

FRENCH GUIANA

GUYANA

Bogota

COLOMBIA

Quito

ECUADOR

Galapagos Islands

River Amazon

BRAZIL

PERU

Lima

Atacama Desert

BOLIVIA

La Paz

Brasilia

Andes

PARAGUAY

Asuncion

São Paulo

Rio de Janeiro

River Paraguay

River Parana

CHILE

Santiago

Mount Aconcagua

ARGENTINA

URUGUAY

Buenos Aires

Montevideo

Andes

Oblique Mercator Projection
© Oxford University Press

In the Amazon rainforest it is very hot and it rains every day. Trees in the forest are being cut down.

Carnaval in Brazil is a street party that lasts for five days.

These giant tortoises live in the Galapagos Islands.

The Amazon rainforest has very many plants, animals and insects.

Angel Falls in Venezuela is the world's highest waterfall.

The Atacama Desert is the driest place in the world. Can you find it on the map?

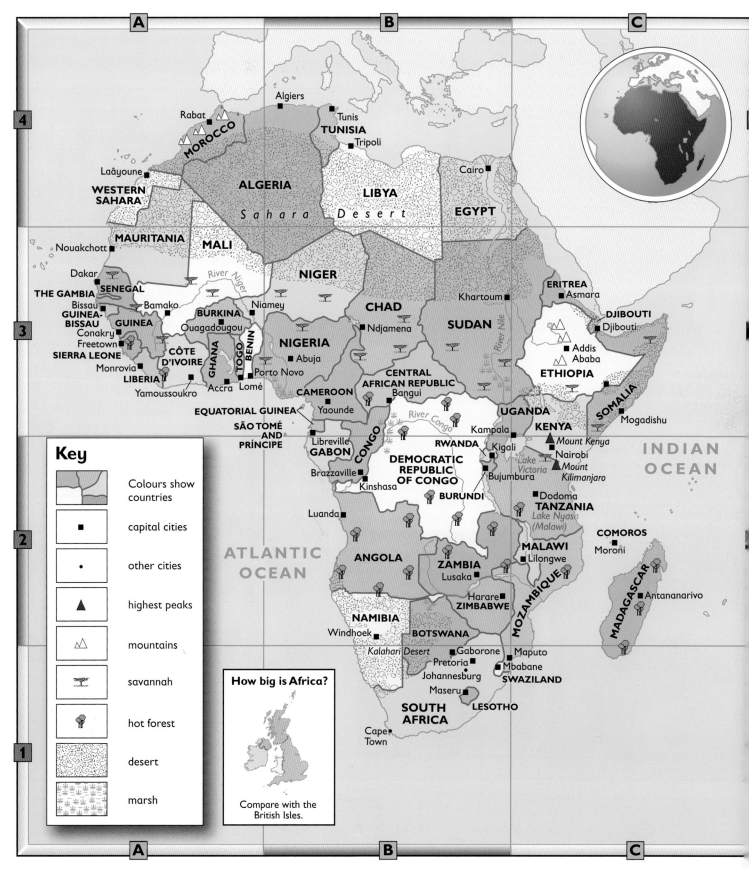

Key

- Colours show countries
- ■ capital cities
- · other cities
- ▲ highest peaks
- ◮ mountains
- savannah
- hot forest
- desert
- marsh

How big is Africa?

Compare with the British Isles.

Algiers
Rabat
TUNISIA
Tunis
MOROCCO
Tripoli
Laâyoune
WESTERN SAHARA
ALGERIA
LIBYA
Cairo
EGYPT
Sahara Desert
Nouakchott
MAURITANIA
MALI
Dakar
River Niger
NIGER
THE GAMBIA
SENEGAL
Bamako
Niamey
ERITREA
Asmara
Khartoum
BISSAU
GUINEA-BISSAU
BURKINA
Ouagadougou
DJIBOUTI
Djibouti
Conakry
GUINEA
Freetown
CÔTE D'IVOIRE
GHANA
TOGO
BENIN
NIGERIA
Abuja
CHAD
Ndjamena
SUDAN
River Nile
Addis Ababa
SIERRA LEONE
Monrovia
LIBERIA
Yamoussoukro
Accra
Lomé
Porto Novo
CAMEROON
CENTRAL AFRICAN REPUBLIC
Bangui
ETHIOPIA
EQUATORIAL GUINEA
Yaounde
River Congo
UGANDA
KENYA
SOMALIA
Mogadishu
SÃO TOMÉ AND PRÍNCIPE
Libreville
GABON
CONGO
Kampala
Mount Kenya
Nairobi
DEMOCRATIC REPUBLIC OF CONGO
RWANDA
Kigali
Lake Victoria
Mount Kilimanjaro
Brazzaville
Kinshasa
BURUNDI
Bujumbura
Dodoma
TANZANIA
INDIAN OCEAN
Luanda
Lake Nyasa (Malawi)
COMOROS
Moroni
ATLANTIC OCEAN
ANGOLA
ZAMBIA
Lusaka
MALAWI
Lilongwe
MADAGASCAR
Antananarivo
MOZAMBIQUE
Harare
ZIMBABWE
NAMIBIA
Windhoek
BOTSWANA
Kalahari Desert
Gaborone
Maputo
Pretoria
Mbabane
Johannesburg
SWAZILAND
SOUTH AFRICA
Maseru
LESOTHO
Cape Town

Zenithal Equal Area Projection
© Oxford University Press

Africa is a continent with many different countries and many different environments.

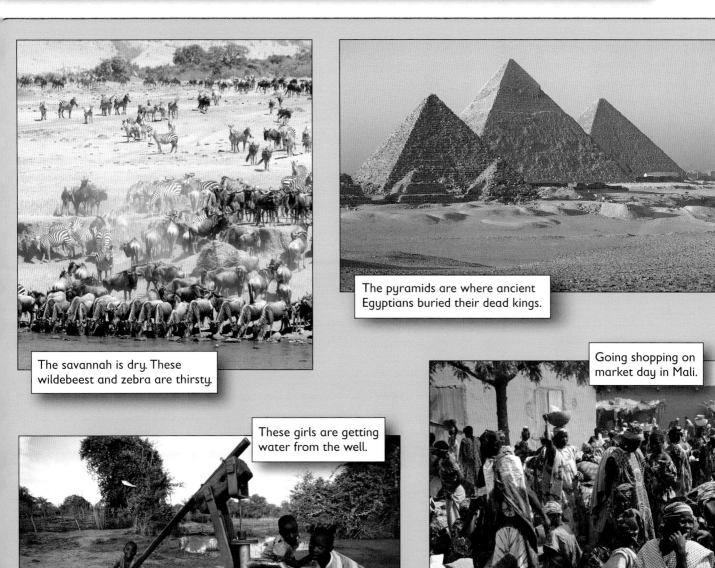

The savannah is dry. These wildebeest and zebra are thirsty.

The pyramids are where ancient Egyptians buried their dead kings.

Going shopping on market day in Mali.

These girls are getting water from the well.

The Sahara Desert is the largest desert in the world. Can you find it on the map?

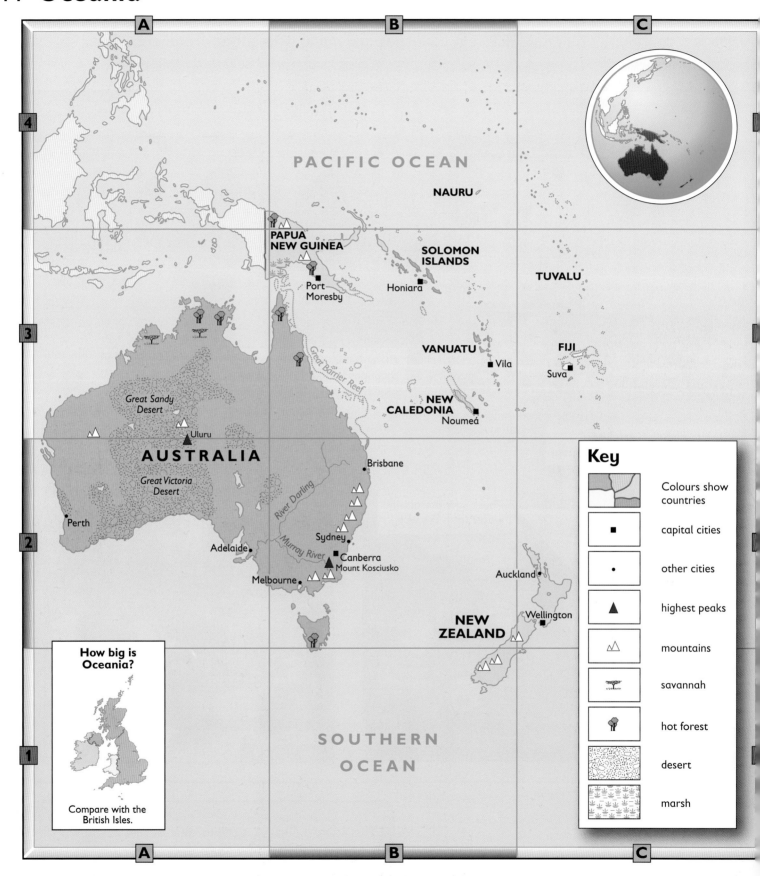

PACIFIC OCEAN

NAURU

PAPUA
NEW GUINEA

SOLOMON
ISLANDS

TUVALU

Port
Moresby

Honiara

VANUATU

FIJI

Vila

Suva

NEW
CALEDONIA

Noumeá

Great Sandy
Desert

Great Barrier Reef

Uluru

AUSTRALIA

Great Victoria
Desert

River Darling

Brisbane

Perth

Sydney

Murray River

Adelaide

Canberra
Mount Kosciusko

Auckland

Melbourne

Wellington

NEW
ZEALAND

SOUTHERN

OCEAN

How big is
Oceania?

Compare with the
British Isles.

Key

(colour blocks)	Colours show countries
■	capital cities
•	other cities
▲	highest peaks
⩍	mountains
(savannah symbol)	savannah
(tree symbol)	hot forest
(desert symbol)	desert
(marsh symbol)	marsh

Modified Gall Projection
© Oxford University Press

Australia is on the other side of the Earth to the British Isles. When it is winter in Britain, it is summer in Australia.

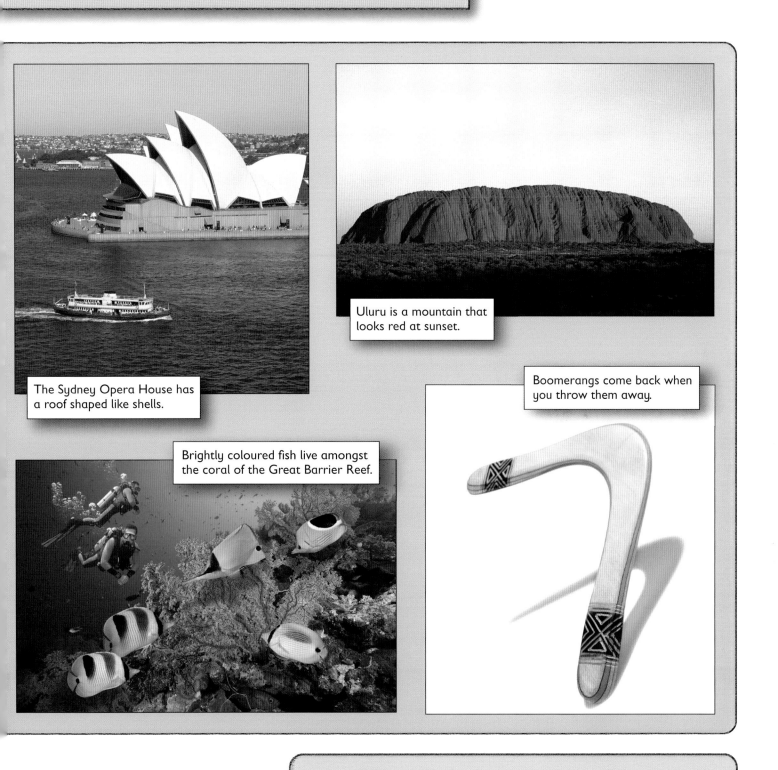

The Sydney Opera House has a roof shaped like shells.

Uluru is a mountain that looks red at sunset.

Boomerangs come back when you throw them away.

Brightly coloured fish live amongst the coral of the Great Barrier Reef.

There are many islands in Oceania. Can you name some of them?

46 Antarctica

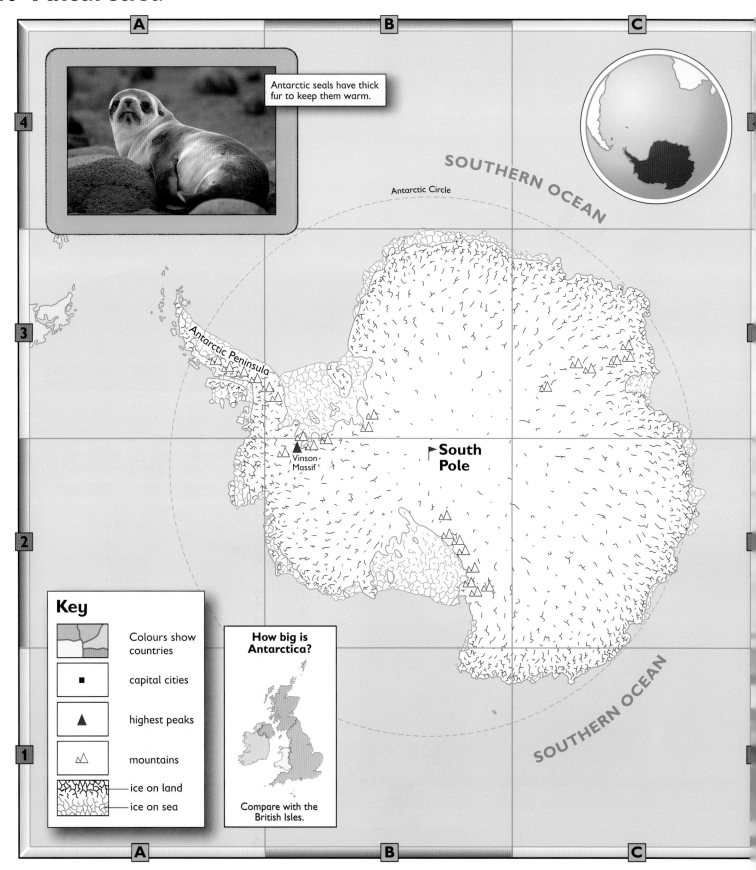

Antarctic seals have thick fur to keep them warm.

SOUTHERN OCEAN

Antarctic Circle

SOUTHERN OCEAN

Antarctic Peninsula

Vinson Massif

▶ **South Pole**

Key

Colours show countries

■ capital cities

▲ highest peaks

△ mountains

ice on land

ice on sea

How big is Antarctica?

Compare with the British Isles.

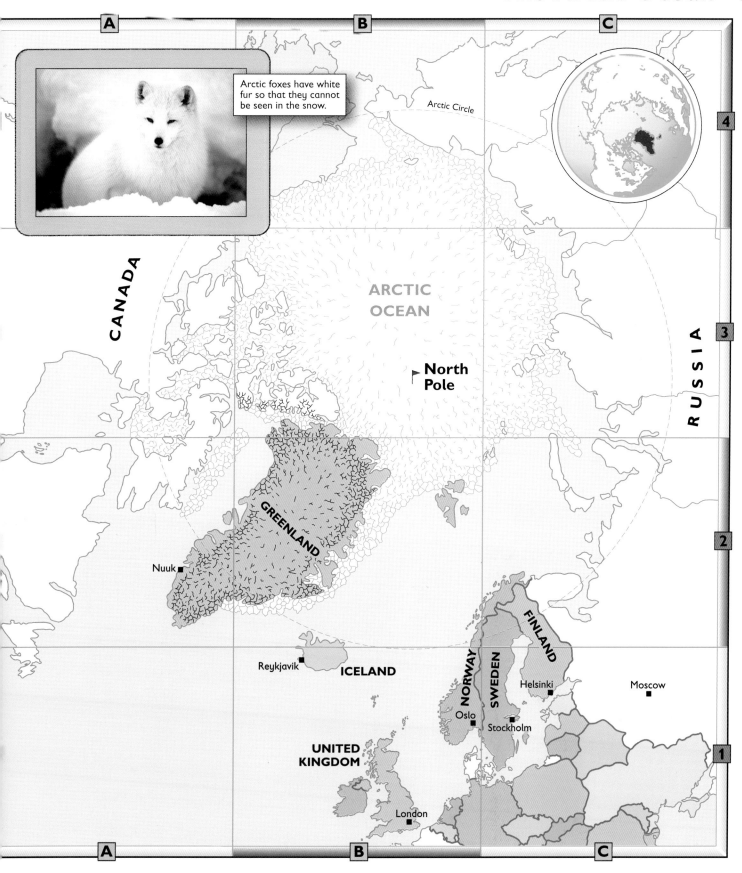

Arctic foxes have white fur so that they cannot be seen in the snow.

Arctic Circle

ARCTIC OCEAN

CANADA

North Pole

GREENLAND

Nuuk

RUSSIA

Reykjavik   ICELAND

NORWAY
SWEDEN
FINLAND

Oslo
Stockholm
Helsinki

Moscow

UNITED KINGDOM

London

A list of some of the most important places in this atlas.

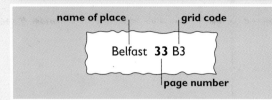

name of place | grid code

Belfast **33** B3

page number